# A Note to Parents

DK READERS is a compelling program for beginning readers, designed in conjunction with leading literacy experts, including Dr. Linda Gambrell, Distinguished Professor of Education at Clemson University. Dr. Gambrell has served as President of the National Reading Conference, the College Reading Association, and the International Reading Association.

Beautiful illustrations and superb full-color photographs combine with engaging, easy-to-read stories to offer a fresh approach to each subject in the series. Each DK READER is guaranteed to capture a child's interest while developing his or her reading skills, general knowledge, and love of reading.

The five levels of DK READERS are aimed at different reading abilities, enabling you to choose the books that are exactly right for your child:

**Pre-level 1**: Learning to read
**Level 1**: Beginning to read
**Level 2**: Beginning to read alone
**Level 3**: Reading alone
**Level 4**: Proficient readers

The "normal" age at which a child begins to read can be

anywhere from three to eight years old. Adult participation through the lower levels is very helpful for providing encouragement, discussing storylines, and sounding out unfamiliar words.

No matter which level you select, you can be sure that you are helping your child learn to read, then read to learn!

LONDON, NEW YORK, MUNICH,
MELBOURNE, AND DELHI

**Publishing Manager, this edition** Bridget Giles
**Executive Editor** Andrea Curley
**Art Director, this edition** Rachael Foster
**Illustrator** Stephen Marchesi

**Reading Consultant**
Linda B. Gambrell, Ph.D.

First American edition, 2001
This edition, 2009
10 11 12 13  10 9 8 7 6 5 4 3 2
Published in the United States by DK Publishing
375 Hudson Street, New York, New York 10014

Published in Great Britain by Dorling Kindersley Limited

DK books are available at special discounts when purchased
in bulk for sales promotions, premiums,
fund-raising, or educational use.
For details, contact: DK Publishing Special Markets
375 Hudson Street, New York, New York 10014
SpecialSales@dk.com

A catalog record for this book is available
from the Library of Congress

ISBN: 978-0-7566-5689-8 (pb)
ISBN: 978-0-7566-5690-4 (plc)

Printed and bound in China by L. Rex Printing Co. Ltd.

The publisher would like to thank the following for
their kind permission to reproduce their photographs:
a=above; b=below/bottom; c=center; l=left; r=right; t=top

*The American Revolution: A Picture Sourcebook*, **Dover
Publications, Inc.:** 10; **Corbis:** Bettmann 36-37, Raymond Gehman
4, Michael Maslan Historic Photographs 5, 6, 12, 16, Annie Griffiths
Belt 17, Richard Hamilton Smith 20, 22, 23, 24, 28, 29, 31, 33, 34,
41, 42, 44, 45, 46, Reinhard Eisele 47; **Getty Images:** fStop / Martin
Hospach 47tr, National Geographic / Rex Stucky 47c; **Library
Of Congress, Washington, D.C.:** 39cr; **The US National Archives
and Records Administration:** 39t
**Front jacket: Getty Images:** Taxi / FPG

All other images © Dorling Kindersley Limited.
For further information see: www.dkimages.com

Discover more at
**www.dk.com**

# Contents

DK READERS

READING
3
ALONE

# Abraham Lincoln

Written by Justine & Ron Fontes

DK Publishing

# Humble beginning

The log cabin's floor was packed dirt. The crude bed was made of poles, corn husks, and bearskins.

The only window looked out on the wilderness of Sinking Spring Farm, near Hodgenville, Kentucky. In this uninspiring setting, on February 12, 1809, Abraham Lincoln was born.

Abe's father, Thomas, could barely write his own name. But the farmer and occasional carpenter was a great storyteller. Abe's mother, Nancy, couldn't read or write at all. But she was a good, kind woman.

*Lincoln cabin replica*

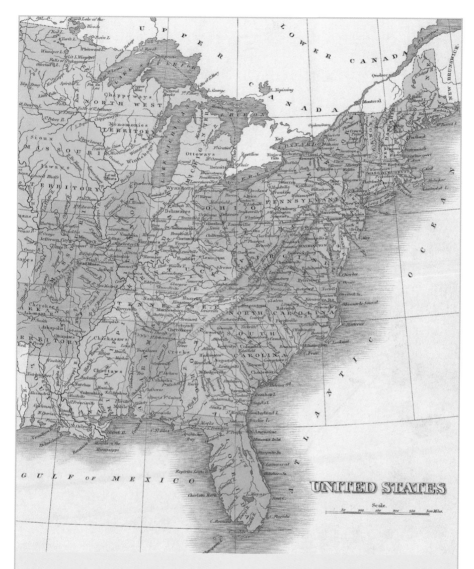

## New nation

When Abe was born, America had only been a country for 33 years. Much of the nation was still unsettled wilderness. There were only 17 states in the union. (Now there are 50.)

The Lincolns soon moved to a farm on the Cumberland Trail, a road used by pioneers. Abe helped with the chores. He also fished, set traps for rabbits and muskrats, and followed bees to their honey trees.

Abe watched the travelers heading West on the trail: Settlers searching for new homes, peddlers, preachers, and sometimes slaves driven South to be sold.

**Southern slaves**
A slave is a person forced to work for someone else. Many southern Americans owned slaves to work their big farms. The slaves were captured in Africa, then brought to slave markets in the U.S.

*Abe went to school in a small, windowless cabin called a "blab school." Students would "blab" their lessons out loud over and over, until they knew them by heart.*

Abe said he went to school "by littles"—a little now and a little then. When there weren't too many chores, Abe and his sister, Sarah, walked many miles to school.

Learning was hard for Abe. But once the shy boy got hold of a new word or idea, Abe knew it forever.

Thomas Lincoln didn't like slavery. So he decided to move to a territory where there were no slaves. They traveled west for two weeks to reach Little Pigeon Creek in Indiana.

Seven-year-old Abe helped clear the family's new land. Abe was skinny, but good with an ax!

That winter, the Lincolns lived in a shelter of poles, brush, and leaves until Thomas built a cabin. They hunted, and also ate honey, nuts, and wild fruit.

Then Nancy got very sick. One day she told Sarah and nine-year-old Abe to be good and kind to their father and each other, and to the world. Then she died! Abe was heartbroken. Without their mother, Abe and Sarah were soon ragged and dirty.

# Learning and lawyers

But Abe wasn't motherless for long. The next year, Thomas married Sally, a widow with three children of her own. They all lived in the cabin, with Abe's orphaned cousin, Dennis, too.

The home was crowded but happy. Even though Sally couldn't read or write, she encouraged Abe's love of learning.

**Heroes from history**

Abe was inspired by the life of George Washington. General Washington commanded the Continental Army during the American Revolution and was the first president of the United States. Abe also admired Benjamin Franklin. As a boy, Franklin was as poor as Abe, but through talent and hard work he became an important inventor and statesman.

*George Washington*

*Benjamin Franklin*

Abe would gladly walk 50 miles to borrow a new book. He copied down ideas he liked and wrote about subjects like cruelty to animals and why American government was great.

Through reading, Abe met heroes like George Washington, people who changed the world.

Abe flew to exciting lands on a magic carpet of words and imagination. He read *The Arabian Nights* to his cousin. Dennis called the exotic adventures "a pack of lies." But, Abe replied, they were "mighty fine lies."

*Scene from* The Arabian Nights

At church, Abe watched the preachers wave their arms. He heard how they raised and lowered their voices to get an audience's attention.

On the way home, Abe would hop on a stump and repeat the sermon word for word. His friends laughed as Abe imitated the preacher's every move.

A stump speaker is a politician who makes informal speeches wherever people gather. Stump speakers used to stand on stumps, like Abe, so they could be seen above the crowd. Abe learned at an early age how to entertain an audience with folksy humor.

*Flatboats were used to ferry cargo or passengers across
shallow water or on rivers. Poles were used to push
flatboats along. Abe poled a flatboat to earn money
when he was a young man.*

Abe heard more speeches when the traveling court came to Booneville, Indiana. A judge and lawyers would travel from town to town to hold trials. Abe listened as the lawyers presented their cases. It never occurred to Abe that he might become a lawyer. Those smart, important men seemed a world away.

Then one day, Abe was poling his flatboat. He took two gentlemen across the river. Each tipped a half-dollar. Abe had never earned so much money so fast. He wondered what else he could do, if he tried.

When Abe was 19, a farmer hired him to take a cargo of goods to New Orleans. There, Abe saw slave markets for the first time. He was horrified.

A few years later, Abe moved to the town of New Salem. He ran a store and became popular because his customers

**Slaves for sale**
At the slave market, people were sold like animals to whoever offered the most money. Families were often separated, never to see their loved ones again.

loved his stories, his kindness, and his honesty.

*Replica of New Salem*

Then the skinny storekeeper took on the county's toughest wrestler. The giant was so impressed by Abe's strength, they became friends. Abe became a hero.

Abe was working hard to be someone important. He convinced the town's schoolmaster to teach him grammar and elocution, the art of speaking clearly. Abe joined the New Salem Debating Society to learn the proper way to present his opinions. He studied law, politics, and history as he always had— in stolen moments, whenever he could. He decided to run for the Illinois state legislature.

Then Indian warriors crossed the Mississippi River to Illinois. White settlers panicked! What if the tribes took back their land?

*Black Hawk was the leader of the Sauk and Fox tribes who briefly invaded Illinois in the Black Hawk War.*

Abe joined the temporary army. His troop elected him captain. Abe made friends with a lawyer named John Todd Stewart. But he never fought anything tougher than mosquitoes or boredom. Like many skirmishes between settlers and Native Americans, the Black Hawk War ended quickly. After the war, Abe had only two weeks to campaign. He lost the election.

Abe wound up working as New Salem's postmaster. Abe met many people through his new job. He decided to campaign again!

Abe used every chance to get votes. He talked to people at dances, house-building parties, and even at wrestling matches. Abe was often the referee because everyone trusted him.

# Victories and vows

*Abe's seat at the state legislature*

This time, Abe won the election and went to the state legislature in Vandalia, Illinois's capital. There Abe renewed his friendship with John Todd Stuart, who was also a lawmaker. Stuart let Abe borrow his law books. Abe studied "by littles" whenever he could. When Abe got his lawyer's license he was invited to join John Stuart's company in Springfield, Illinois.

Abe campaigned to move the Illinois capital to Springfield. He wanted his new town to be an important place. Before long, Springfield was the capital—and Abe was at the center of Illinois politics!

Abe spoke out against slavery and lynch mobs, the crowds who hunted down and hanged escaped slaves. But Abe was not one of the "abolitionists" trying to ban slavery. Abe believed the government should keep new territories free, not try to abolish slavery where it already existed.

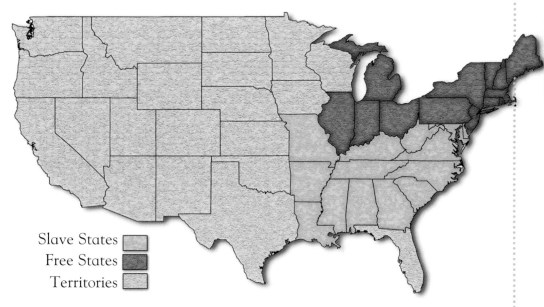

Slave States
Free States
Territories

*When Abe first spoke out against slavery, all the Southern and a few Northern states were slave states. There was great debate about whether slavery should be allowed in new territories.*

Abe was a busy lawyer of 30 when he met a woman who seemed his opposite. Abe was tall, thin, awkward, and unrefined. Mary Todd was short, plump, stylish, and charming. He came from a log cabin. She had been raised in luxury,

### Lincoln's look

Abe's rumpled clothes made it clear to people that his mind was on more important things than fashion. His long legs poked from his plain pant legs. His boots were dusty from walking. Abe carried his papers in a tall stovepipe hat that made him seem even taller than his 6'4". Once people met him, they never forgot Abe!

*Mary Todd opposed slavery, but her father owned slaves on his large farm in Kentucky. Mary happened to be the cousin of Abe's lawyer friend, John Todd Stuart.*

and attended fancy private schools. Mary spoke French and knew all the latest dance steps.

But beneath the surface, Abe and Mary had much in common. Both cared deeply about justice, politics, and poetry. And both had lost their mothers at a young age.

By the time Abe was 33, he had realized that Mary Todd was the woman for him. Mary was very popular, but she chose Abe.

They got married on November 4, 1842, and started saving to buy a house. Within a year, Abe had a son, Robert, and had bought his first home, a cottage on a nice street in Springfield.

The Lincolns added rooms to their cottage, and Mary gave birth to another son. But Eddy died when he was not quite four. Shortly after his death, Mary gave birth to William, and then Thomas,

*The Lincoln home in Springfield, Illinois*

who became known as Tad. Abe doted on his boys, especially little Tad. Mary loved them, too, but she never quite got over Eddy's death.

*Abe and Tad*

# On the move

Abe was elected to Congress, so the Lincolns moved to Washington, D.C. Abe saw slave markets in the country's capital. The Constitution said all men are created equal. How could people be sold like animals?

Abe proposed a law to abolish slavery in Washington. The law did not pass, and Abe lost his second term. Ending slavery would not be easy.

Abe went back to Springfield, but soon joined the 8th Circuit Court. This traveling court brought justice to small towns, like the trials he'd seen as a young man.

Abe spent half the year sleeping on farmhouse floors or sharing beds in crowded taverns. Between cases the lawyers joked, sang, and played cards. Abe could forget fancy manners and help simple folk!

*The 8th Circuit Court served the entire state of Illinois. The judge, Abe, and the other lawyers traveled 500 miles on horseback, then on the newly built railroads.*

The work was challenging. The lawyers rode into town, found clients, then presented their cases right away.

One time, in New Salem, Abe was asked to defend an old friend named Duff, who was accused of murder. The witness claimed he saw Duff kill by the light of the full moon. But, with an almanac, Abe proved the moon was just a sliver on that night, so the witness was lying. Duff was free by nightfall.

**Fact book**

An almanac is a book of information about a given year. It tells the times of sunrise and sunset for that year, as well as cycles of the moon. Farmers can use an almanac to predict the weather and decide when to plant crops.

*Abe had spent his whole life learning to speak. He was not a handsome man and his voice was shrill. But when Abe spoke, the power of his emotions shone in his eyes and people were moved.*

Abe was a happy lawyer. But he wanted to help make sure slavery didn't spread into the new territories. So he ran for the Senate.

Abe gave a speech calling America "a house divided." He said, "…this government cannot endure, permanently half slave and half free. It will become all one thing, or all the other."

Abe's opponent was a famous politician named Stephen A. Douglas. Douglas saw no need to outlaw slavery in the new territories, since the land wasn't right for tobacco, cotton, or other slave crops. Abe thought Congress had to preserve the new states as "places for poor people to go and better their condition."

Abe suggested a series of debates. The result was America's greatest duel of words!

Abe lost the election, but won acclaim. Just as he had wrestled the strongest man in New Salem, Abe had battled a political giant and proved himself a man worth watching. And by forcing Douglas to take a public stand, Abe made slavery the issue of the day.

Douglas was a well-dressed, well-fed statesman who traveled to each debate in his own private railroad car. Abe arrived in the crowded public train and then rode a haywagon to his hotel. The two candidates were as different as a purebred poodle and a farmyard hound.

Just two years later, in 1860, the Republican party chose Abe to run for president. Abe had helped form the new party, but did not expect this honor.

**Party politics**
The Republican party was created in Illinois in 1856. They favored rule by representation, rather than direct vote. During Lincoln's time there were several other political parties, including the

*Republican party symbol*

Democrats, Whigs, and Constitutional Union. The Democratic party was founded in 1830 on the principles of government by the people and equal rights for all. Created in 1836, the Whig party opposed the Democrats until it dissolved in 1856. Originally, Whigs were those who supported the American Revolution.

*Democratic party symbol*

Springfield went wild. A Republican parade that passed the Lincoln home contained so many people, it took 8 hours to pass the house.

There were more than two candidates running for president that year. Abe received only 40% of the votes, but he won!

*Election poster showing Abe with his running mate, Hannibal Hamlin.*

However, Abe lost in every Southern state. Newspapers raged against Lincoln's anti-slavery stance. They even urged the South to prepare for war.

# A house divided

Abe had come a long way from the shy schoolboy, the New Salem storekeeper, and the defeated congressman. Now he was president of the United States.

**The Confederate States of America**
Alabama, Florida, Georgia, Louisiana, Mississippi and Texas joined South Carolina to make up the first seven states in the Confederate States of America. Jefferson Davis was elected as their president.

But even as Abe rode the presidential train from Springfield to the White House, the United States stopped being united. South Carolina left the Union, followed by six other Southern states. They called themselves the Confederate States of America. They

raised a flag, adopted a slavery-protecting constitution, and elected their own president.

People in many Confederate states wanted Abe dead. Though crowds still cheered at every station, Abe's journey had become dangerous. When his train reached Washington, D.C., Abe took off his stovepipe hat and sneaked into the White House in disguise.

On his first night in the White House, Abe learned that Confederate warships and cannons were threatening Fort Sumter, a Union fort in South Carolina. To make things worse, Fort Sumter was running out of supplies.

Should Abe risk war by sending troops? Should he send food and guns so

the fort could defend itself? Could the troops somehow just leave?

Abe asked his advisors, but they all said different things. Abe paced the White House. He wanted to avoid a war. Finally, he decided to send supplies. Then Confederate troops bombed Fort Sumter. The Civil War had begun.

Abe thought the war would end quickly. Instead, blood soaked the land for weeks, months, and years. Abe's generals somehow never won. They always stopped short of complete victory. Abe chose new generals, but they also proved timid.

Abe knew about war only from books and his three months fighting mosquitoes and boredom in the Black Hawk War. What should he do?

Then Abe's 11-year-old son, Willie, caught a mysterious fever. The doctors were at a loss. Mary was frantic! Eight-year-old Tad also got sick. The president was weighed down with worry. His only relief was going to the theater. There he could watch a play and forget his problems for a short time.

## Free frontier

Most of Abe's presidency was taken up with the Civil War. But he also helped tame the West. On May 20, 1862, Abe approved the Federal Homestead Act, which offered Western land free to anyone brave or desperate enough to settle in the wild territory. Thousands rushed across the Mississippi River to stake their claims and dig their destiny in free soil.

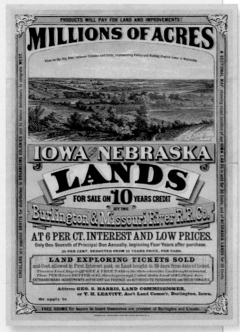

*Poster advertising free, undeveloped land in the West.*

# Pain then Union

Willie died in February. Mary was too sad to even go to the funeral. Tad got better, but the war dragged on. Seven months after Willie's death, on September 17, 1862, America suffered its bloodiest day.

In the Battle of Antietam, Maryland, nearly 5,000 men died and over 20,000 were wounded. The Union won the battle, but no one felt like celebrating.

On January 1, 1863, Abe's Emancipation Proclamation was passed.

*Civil War medicine was crude. Pain killers were rare. Doctors were very excited by the new discovery that washing their hands between operations could reduce the spread of germs.*

*President Lincoln reads a draft of the Emancipation Proclamation to his cabinet.*

Emancipation means "to set free." A proclamation is a formal statement.

Abolitionists hated Abe's Emancipation Proclamation because it only freed slaves in the South and let Northern blacks join the Union army. Southerners thought Abe had no right to tell them what to do. He wasn't even their president anymore!

On July 4, 1863, the Union won a great victory at Gettysburg, Pennsylvania. But so many men died that it seemed better to build a national cemetery on the spot than ship all the bodies home.

At the cemetery's dedication on November 19, 1863, Abe gave his most

### The Gettysburg Address

"Four score and seven years ago our fathers brought forth on this continent, a new nation, conceived in Liberty, and dedicated to the proposition that all men are created equal.

Now we are engaged in a great civil war, testing whether that nation, or any nation so conceived and so dedicated, can long endure. We are met on a great battle-field of that war. We have come to dedicate a portion of that field, as a final resting place for those who here gave their lives that that nation might live. It is altogether fitting and proper that we should do this.

But, in a larger sense, we can not dedicate—we can not consecrate—we can not hallow—this ground. The brave men, living and dead, who struggled here, have consecrated it, far above our poor power to add or detract. The world will little note, nor long remember what we say here, but it can never forget what they did here. It is for us the living, rather, to be dedicated here to the unfinished work which they who fought here have thus far so nobly advanced. It is rather for us to be here dedicated to the great task remaining before us—that from these honored dead we take increased devotion to that cause for which they gave the last full measure of devotion—that we here highly resolve that these dead shall not have died in vain—that this nation, under God, shall have a new birth of freedom—and that government of the people, by the people, for the people, shall not perish from the earth."

**Thanks, Abe**

On October 3, 1863, Abe issued a proclamation setting aside "…the last Thursday of November next as a day of Thanksgiving and praise…" This national holiday is still celebrated.

famous speech. The Gettysburg Address lasted less than three minutes and touched on a topic from one of Abe's blab school essays: The sacredness of American government.

Abe wanted to make the Union whole again. He also pushed for an addition (called an amendment) to the Constitution that would abolish slavery in America. The 13th Amendment would succeed where the Emancipation Proclamation had failed.

Abe ran for a second term and was re-elected in 1864. He won a vast

*For the entire day after the Southern surrender, crowds outside the White House serenaded Abe. The president asked the band to play the Southern anthem, "Dixie." Abe said it was "one of the best tunes I have ever heard."*

majority, but still received hate mail and threats.

Still, Abe achieved his goals: On January 31, 1865, the 13th Amendment officially ended slavery in America. And on April 9th, the South surrendered. A few nights later, Abe and Mary went to Ford's Theatre to enjoy a comedy. But as they laughed, an angry actor plotted tragedy. John Wilkes Booth and his friends thought Abe had ruined America, and only his death would save the South. So during the play, Booth sneaked up behind Abe and shot him in the head.

*John Wilkes Booth makes his escape after shooting the President.*

Abe never opened his eyes again. He died early the next morning.

On April 21, 1865, Abe began a journey that would almost exactly reverse his 1860 trip to the White House. The nine-car funeral train stopped in eleven cities as it chugged slowly across the country.

*Abe's funeral train*

Along the way, America mourned with gunshots, bonfires, songs, prayers, and flowers.

The nation cried for a man who had given his life to preserving the ideal of freedom—as Abe said in the Gettysburg Address, "…that government of the people, by the people, for the people, shall not perish from the earth."

The 20-foot-tall statue of Abe inside the Lincoln Memorial is made of 28 blocks of white marble fitted together so expertly that it looks like one piece. Each year, more than four million people visit the Lincoln Memorial in Washington, D.C.

# Glossary

**Abolitionist**
Someone seeking to "abolish" slavery. Abolish means to eliminate or end.

**Almanac**
A year-by-year book of data about the motion of the stars and planets, including the phases of the moon.

**Amendment**
An addition or other change to a law or constitution. The 13th Amendment to the U.S. Constitution set free all America's slaves.

**Candidate**
A person who seeks to be elected to an office, like President of the United States.

**Circuit court**
Originally, a judge and lawyers who traveled a district holding court in various towns.

**Civil war**
War between different groups within one country. The American Civil War was fought between the North (the Union) and the South (the Confederacy) from 1861 to 1865.

**Confederate**
A group united by a common purpose. The Confederate States of America were the eleven Southern states that left the Union between December 1860 and June 1861.

**Constitution**
A document describing the basic laws and principles of a country (or other group).

**Debate**
A formal argument, often used to discuss political or legal issues; a duel of words.

**The Emancipation Proclamation**
The January 1, 1863, Emancipation Proclamation was a law that freed some of the slaves in America.

**Legislator**
A member of a legislature, which is the group of people responsible for making laws in an area, such as a state.

**Political party**
A group of people with similar ideas about government. Political parties support candidates for office.

**Republican**
One of the two major political parties in the United States. The Republican party was organized in 1856 in a failed attempt to prevent the election of James Buchanan to the presidency.

**Senator**
A member of the Senate. The Senate and House of Representatives make up one of the three branches of the American government. Senators are elected to represent their home states.

**Slavery**
The practice of owning slaves, which means keeping, buying, and selling human beings for the purpose of forcing them to work against their will and not for their own benefit.